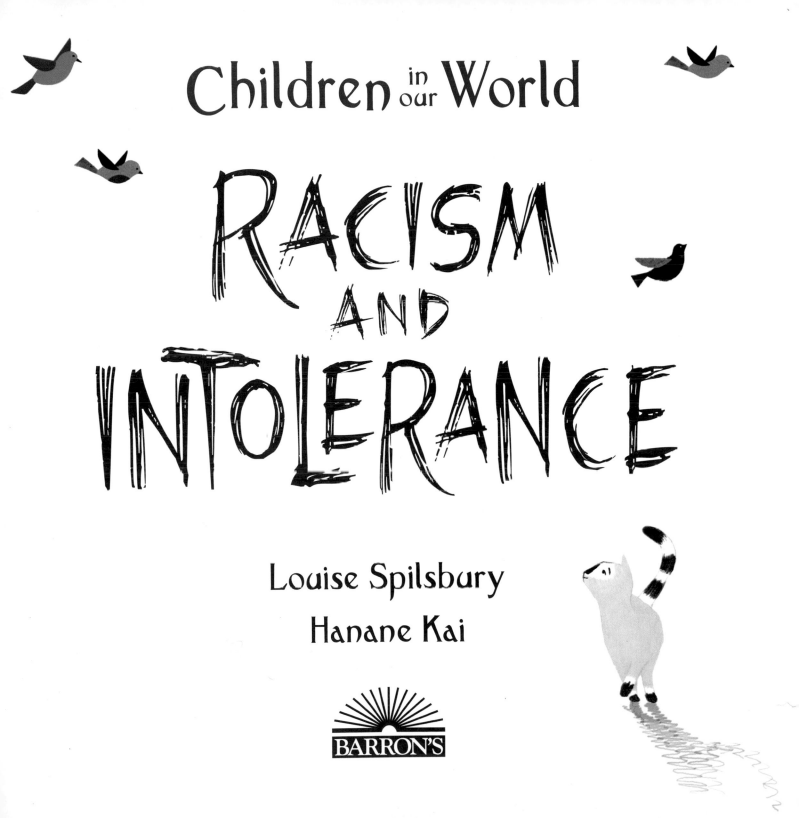

Children in our World

RACISM AND INTOLERANCE

Louise Spilsbury

Hanane Kai

BARRON'S

First edition for the United States and Canada published in 2018
by Barron's Educational Series, Inc.

First published in Great Britain in 2017 by Wayland

Wayland is an imprint of Hachette Children's Books, part of Hodder & Stoughton.
A Hachette U.K. company.
www.hachette.co.uk
www.hachettechildrens.co.uk

Text © Hodder & Stoughton, 2017
Written by Louise Spilsbury
Illustrations © Hanane Kai, 2017

Texturing of illustrations by Sarah Habli
Edited by Corinne Lucas
Designed by Sophie Wilkins

All inquiries should be addressed to:
Barron's Educational Series, Inc.
250 Wireless Boulevard
Hauppauge, NY 11788
www.barronseduc.com

ISBN: 978-1-4380-5022-5

Library of Congress Control No.: 2017944950

Date of Manufacture: November 2017
Manufactured by: WKT Co., Ltd., Shenzhen, China

Printed in China
9 8 7 6 5 4 3 2 1

The website addresses (URLs) included in this book were valid at the time of going to press.
However, it is possible that contents or addresses may have changed since the publication of this
book. No responsibility for any such changes can be accepted by either the author or the Publisher.

Contents

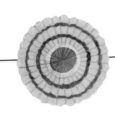

Living together

The world is made up of all types of people. We like different foods, play different sports, and have different hobbies. Most of us live happily side by side. We get to know each other and act with kindness and respect.

Sadly, some people do not always treat others fairly. They may be very unkind to people they think are different from them.

What is racism?

Sometimes people are treated differently because of the color of their skin, their family background, or the country they come from. This is known as racism.

Racism is a form of prejudice. Prejudice is when you dislike particular groups of people without knowing them. Imagine disliking someone before you have spoken to or know anything about him or her. Does that sound fair?

What is intolerance?

Some people are intolerant of those who live a different way of life from them. Intolerance is when people do not accept someone else's family, home, religion, or lifestyle because it is different from theirs.

PRIORITY SEATING
FOR ELDERLY
AND DISABLED

Intolerance can take many forms. One type is when people speak badly about other religions, or when they treat people from a different religion unfairly. Everyone should be able to follow the faith they choose, without being hated.

PRIORITY SEATING
FOR ELDERLY
AND DISABLED

What causes prejudice?

People can become prejudiced when one person from a group does something bad or wrong. They start to believe that everyone from that group is bad, even though that is not fair or true.

Sometimes people are unkind to others who look or act different from them. Even if you disagree with someone's beliefs, you should still respect his or her way of life.

At school

At school, students might make a joke about another student's religion. They may call other students nasty names or leave them out of games because they speak different languages or look different from them.

Being treated differently because of your race or religion is never funny or fair. It can make you feel alone, angry, and scared. Some children may be too upset to concentrate in class or to go to school. It can even make them feel sick.

Around the world

People who are racist and intolerant may shout at, threaten, or hurt other people. They might paint bad words on people's homes or places of worship, or even bomb buildings.

Some people are told they cannot live in certain places or do certain jobs, or they may be paid less money because of the color of their skin or their beliefs. They may be told they cannot wear certain clothes. How would you feel if that happened to you?

15

Changing lives

Racism and intolerance create a world where people do not trust and respect each other. They stir up bad feelings and hatred. This hatred can cause fighting and lead to wars.

Some people are killed because of their race or their religion. In some countries, families are forced to leave their homes. They try to escape to a new place where they hope to live in safety and peace.

People who help

Many people across the world work hard to stop racism and intolerance. Countries have laws to stop people from being refused jobs or from being treated unfairly.

A charity is a group that helps people. Some charity workers help to get fair treatment for people affected by racism and intolerance. They try to teach people why racism and intolerance are wrong, what problems they cause, and the harm they do.

Keeping people safe

Rules keep us safe. Schools have strict rules about racism. In some countries, schools keep records of any racist bullying that happens. Teachers have steps to follow if a student is treated unfairly because of racism or intolerance.

The police can take action to protect people from racism and intolerance, too. They can make reports about people who shout angry insults or hurt others. They can even arrest and imprison them.

Respecting differences

Tolerance means respecting others for their differences. We are all different from each other in some way. You might not think the way you look or do things is different or unusual because you are used to them. But, we all appear different to others.

Differences are what make the world an interesting place. If someone at your school comes from another country, why not ask them about it? To learn about other beliefs, maybe you could invite a friend to celebrate one of your traditions, and then share in one of theirs.

Things that unite us

We are all much more alike than we are different. We all need food, water, clothes, and homes to live in. We all need to learn, work, and have fun in our lives. We all laugh and cry, and we like to spend time with our families and friends. We all need to be free and safe.

When you meet someone new, try to find things you have in common and respect any differences. Do you like the same subjects at school? Do you like the same music, jokes, games, or movies? Finding the things that connect us can be fun.

Talk about it

Racism and intolerance make a lot of people angry and upset.
If you feel worried or sad, talk to an adult you trust.
He or she can help you to feel better. If you have
been bullied because of your race, culture, or
beliefs, tell an adult right away.

Racism and intolerance are wrong and unfair. But remember, there
are many people, of all races and religions, working to make things
better. Most people around the world are tolerant and caring.

How can you help?

You can help change attitudes by learning and sharing information about other cultures and religions. If you see someone being treated badly or unfairly because of their race or culture, make sure they are okay, and then tell an adult you trust.

You could also sell old toys or put on a show to raise money for charities and groups that work to stop racism and intolerance. Or, you could help your teacher create a world culture day at school.

Find out more

If you are a victim of racism or intolerance, it is very important that you tell an adult about how you are being treated.

Books

Whoever You Are
Mem Fox, Reading Rainbow Books, 2006

I'm Like You, You're Like Me: A Book About Understanding and Appreciating Each Other
Cindy Gainer, Free Spirit Publishing, 2013

Separate Is Never Equal: Sylvia Mendez and Her Family's Fight for Desegregation
Duncan Tonatiuh, Harry N. Abrams, 2014

Websites

Youth for Human Rights International (YHRI) teaches youth about human rights and inspires them to become advocates for peace.
www.youthforhumanrights.org

STOMP Out Bullying is an anti-bullying organization for kids and teens in the U.S. that focuses on preventing bullying, deterring violence in schools, and educating against racism and hatred of all kinds.
www.stompoutbullying.org

The Respect Diversity Foundation promotes tolerance and acceptance through communication, education, and the arts.
www.therespectdiversityfoundation.org

The Canadian Anti-racism Education and Research Society offers anti-racism workshops and training in non-violent solutions to racism and hate group activity.
www.stopracism.ca

Glossary

charity a group that helps people in need

culture the beliefs, values, and ways of behaving and celebrating that a particular group of people share

intolerance refusing to accept views, beliefs, or behaviors that are different from your own

laws rules that people must follow

prejudice disliking a person or group simply because they belong to a particular race, religion, or different group

race a group of people who may come from the same place, share the same language, and look similar in some way

racism treating people differently based on the color of their skin, their family background, or the country they come from

religion a belief in a god or gods, for example, Islam and Christianity

respect to care about other people's feelings and opinions

tolerance the ability to accept views, ways of life, or beliefs that are different from your own

worship to show respect for a god, for example, to pray

Index

31901063465688